The Game Plan: Becoming a Top Performing Leader

Gene Howell

The Game Plan: Becoming a
Top Performing Leader

Published in 2011
by Gene Howell

Book cover design and layout
by Publicious Pty Ltd
www.publicious.com.au

Catalogue-in-Publication details available
from the National Library of Australia

ISBN: 978-0-9872221-3-8

Contents

Acknowledgements

I would like to acknowledge the many people who have made me what I am today through my being with or learning from them, both here in Australia and overseas.

But special thanks must go to two individuals who have influenced how I see leadership:

•   Patrick Cullen, Executive Director of the Australian Institute of Management, WA – I believe he has made AIM what it is today, and to serve under him for the past 10 years has been a real learning experience. He set the tone for "Having lunch with your future" and insight into what great leadership should and shouldn't be.

•   Dr Shaun Ridley, Deputy Executive Director of AIMWA, who has been my immediate manager and mentor. I thank him especially for the many in-depth conversations and challenges he has held with me and the inspirational leadership he continues to offer. Both Patrick and Shaun make the Institute one of the most inspirational, enjoyable and exciting places in which to work.

Lastly, my special thanks go to Zion Praise Harvest Church for their belief in and support of me over the past years – they continue to help develop some of the best future professional leaders in Australia.

FOREWORD

by Patrick Cullen
Executive Director Australian Institute
of Management Western Australia

It is a great pleasure to write this foreword for Gene's book, particularly given it is on the important topic of leadership. So much has been written over the years on the subject of management and leadership, but rarely has a book been written that is easy to read and yet full of wisdom and practical advice on how to make the most of your leadership potential. This is such a book.

Sometimes we think about leadership in terms of a title and we often think about leadership as the domain of a few senior executives who exist in an organisation. However, every person has leadership potential regardless of their place in an organisational hierarchy. The extent to which this potential is used varies significantly – sometimes by choice, sometimes by lack of awareness and knowledge. Gene's insights will hopefully give each reader some additional knowledge, including some tips and advice that if applied skilfully can help in a significant way to build confidence and further leverage that leadership potential that exists within us. If we can all better leverage our leadership capacity, think about the impact that might have in our private and personal life!

Gene has worked in the management and leadership space for many years, including a significant period of time in community youth leadership development roles. Most recently he has worked as a senior executive developing and delivering management and leadership programs for the Australian Institute of Management Western Australia. Gene has leveraged this experience to not only grow and develop his own leadership style, but also to facilitate the further development of all who attend his sessions. He has a wealth of real life experience and some of that experience is shared openly in this book.

The Australian Institute of Management Western Australia has been privileged to have Gene work with us over many years, helping to improve the performance of managers and leaders at all levels in organisations. I hope this book helps to improve your performance through unleashing some of the leadership potential within.

Patrick Cullen.
2011.

The Author's Comment

Leadership has always interested me. First as a young boy, watching with awe those who seemed to be in the limelight - the singers, the talkers, the conference speakers. As I grew into my teens, it was the super idols - the famous singers and speakers, the book writers, the TV actors. Growing still older, it became the well-known whom I admired - still the speakers, the politicians who led the country, the people who reported the news, the rich and famous who more and more seemed to live in our house through the medium of TV.

Then one day I started to meet such people myself, and was able to see what others didn't see - the humanness behind them rather than the aura I had always associated with them. Some of what I saw I liked; some of it I didn't. I stood backstage as one singer was about to go on stage and sing a particularly moving song - they said to me in an aside "I hate this song!" then as they were announced and ran on stage, proceeded to tell people how this was their favourite song and what it meant to them. On the other hand, in another time and place, I watched as a well-known speaker finished talking and the minders moved in to protect him and stop people from rushing him. He stopped them and moved out to speak to people and greet them and answer questions.

It made me think about what it is that makes a good leader.

I sat with Cliff Richard over lunch one day when he was on tour, he had just left a press conference he'd invited me to attend and we had both gone down to the hotel restaurant to eat. Several times through the meal, people came up and interrupted us, asking for an autograph, or just to say how great they thought he was. I watched as he responded each time as if this was the time of his life, that he was just waiting for someone to interrupt. He responded so well, so friendly and openly. I asked him afterwards if it ever annoyed him, and his response was interesting "I always remind myself that these are the very people who put me here, who pay to see me in concert, who buy my CDs. Why would I annoy the people who put me where I am?"

Great question and even better answer. As someone once said: "Be careful who you step on, on the way up, because one day they could be the people who pass you on your way down!" yet I have seen many things happen in leadership that break both of the above comments, and has proven to be the downfall of many a leader, simply because they ignored the people who had put them there.

These days I mainly train people in leadership, and tend to centre on a few examples - the Richard Bransons of the world, or the Sydney surgeon Charlie Teo (who I will talk more about later)...and sometimes people closer to home - sometimes the silent, not so well known ones, who maybe will never rate the news, but still manage to impact people's lives around them in their quiet ways.

Being involved in this training and learning at the Institute, researching material for leadership and management programs, and seeking out new or different ways to impact people through these learning experiences has made me think long and hard about the whole area of leadership. One thing I have noticed is that many of the books we have written in this area are like the famous war books – they are always written from the point of view of the people who won. So I have purposely set out to try and provide a practical book that gives you insight into areas of leadership we don't always talk about – things like where does a leader get their power from, do we need to consider a person's spirituality, or how to identify what's called 'the UGR's' in a workplace, amongst a few. Don't worry – I'll explain that one later!

These and many other questions have bothered me over the years as I have learned about and grown into leadership, and they are questions that often come up on programs I run. I felt that it was time to write some of these things down so that people who don't get to attend any of the programs run at the Institute can at least have some inkling of what they need to consider as they enter a pathway that leads to leadership in their workplace. And by the way, if you haven't yet attended a training program at the Australian Institute of Management Western Australia, maybe you should, as we offer some of the best learning experiences you will ever encounter! I may be biased, but that's how I see their programs…

So I want to share with you some lessons on leadership in this book, some of which I have learned personally, some of which I have observed and learned from others along the journey, adding the lessons to my own repertoire. I think if I had the courage, I would title this book "21 lessons on leadership you need to learn but they never taught you so watch out because if you ignore them it's really going to mess you up!"

However, it's probably better if I title this book "The Game Plan: Becoming a Top Performing Leader", because that's really what it is about. This is about the skills, knowledge and attitude you need, to be the top leader you can be. This is not about what you are now; it's about what you will become.

Gene Howell
2011

CHAPTER 1
What does a leader look like?

I have been working for the Australian Institute of Management for the past ten years. I started as a consultant on an 18 month contract with a specific task at hand. I progressed to a management level. The role grew, until I began to feel overpowered by it. So nine years down the track, when another job opportunity arose within AIM, I went for it, much to the surprise of Patrick, the ED.

Over lunch, he asked me why I was going for this other job, a role in which he just could not see me as being suited. I explained that I knew I needed a change, that I was feeling stressed by the demands of the work which seemed to have grown and grown to the point where I was feeling as if I were unable to do anything fully to the level to which I wanted to attain.

In his book "Good to Great", author Jim Collins talks about the different levels of leadership. The highest level is Level 5. Here the leader isn't about posing and setting themselves up as the saviour of the company, the 'lone ranger riding over the mountain to save everyone'; rather, at Level 5 this leader is about engaging others, including them in the circle of influence, giving recognition to the collectiveness of those around them.

WHAT DOES A LEADER LOOK LIKE?

One of the concepts that Collins also talks about is having "the right people on the bus". He follows this through with the idea that people aren't your best asset - the right *people* are your best asset!

So how far do you go to keep the right people? This is where good leadership comes in. A good leader recognises the people who will work with them to achieve the goals they have set. A good leader works with the right people. And a good leader keeps the right people engaged.

That's why I regard Patrick as a good leader. Instead of letting me go, because I certainly wasn't achieving what I was supposed to, he created another role for me to live in to. It was a role which still achieved for the Institute, yet it also used the strengths I have as well. Over the time I have been there, I have watched him do the same with other people whom he considered had a valuable contribution to make to the Institute.

That's what leadership is about - correction, that's what *good* or *great* leadership is about.

Now the question of how a leader should act or what they should look like is an interesting one. This almost supposes that there is a form or certain character that leaders should have, but this is so incorrect as to be almost laughable.

Apparently, one of the most leader-looking Presidents of the USA was President Warren Harding. He looked like what a leader should look like in people's opinions. Commanding, strong features, honest and deep set eyes, firm grip, handsome, tall, well-built, strong voice - in fact, it appears he was a marketing manager's dream come true. It also seems, from what we can ascertain, that he became President because of those very characteristics. He looked like a President. When people looked at him, they saw leader.

Appearances aren't all they are cooked up to be. And this was especially true of Harding. When elected, with a huge majority of the popular vote, he proved to be other than a leader. He made no major decisions, no major speeches (except for what the Party had him trot out), and found it difficult to make his mind up. He is constantly relegated to being regarded as the worst President the United States have ever had! Ouch!

There are no special looks that distinguish leaders, but there are principles that usually show through.

In "The Leadership Challenge" (Kouzes and Posner), the authors point out that their research shows some four principles make a good leader. Their research has carried them around the world, and they check their research and renew the findings every three or four years or so, so it keeps it current. They offer a 360 degree questionnaire to help people determine how others see them as a leader. It is a fantastic tool to use, but it can also be devastating when you see how other people see you. When I use this tool, I have to remind people before they look at their results that it is another person's perception of them, rather than true reality. Sometimes people can be devastated by how others see them.

Kouzes and Posner help people identify their strengths and weaknesses and then plan how to address the weaknesses. Marcus Buckingham (author of "True North" and other books) suggests another approach, as we will discuss later. But his suggestion of looking more to the strengths rather than your weakness makes a lot of sense when you read his context. What these two authors alone show us is that even writers on leadership differ as to what true leaders should look like or what they concentrate on. I have mentioned Jim Collins and his book "Good to Great" and it seems to me that Buckingham has disagreement with Collins as well in this area. The more writers we look at, the more variance we seem to find.

I have only ever come across one writer who dared to suggest that leaders do look a certain way. In fact, he even suggested that they would be a certain height, that no short person could ever hold a significant position of leadership (he obviously disregarded such leaders as Ghandi, Gold Meir, Mussolini, Nehru, Chairman Mao, to name but a few). I never saw a picture of the writer, and I now cannot even remember his name (for which I am very thankful), but it would be interesting to see what he looked like! Probably short, and writing to compensate!

I don't think there is some magical formula that will show you what a leader should look like. And the now deceased President Harding is a good example of someone who held all the supposed looks of a leader, but in the end, wasn't considered a good leader.

When I was at school, one of my close friends was a top athlete. Brilliant at any sport he chose, whether swimming or running, football, or cricket, he was fantastic. He also had the looks, blond hair, green eyes, handsome, and well built. The world was on his plate. He took part in inter-school athletics, and was in the State Athletics Team. I envied him, because I was the exact opposite! I wanted what he had. A couple of times, he stayed over at my place, and we had fun just as friends normally do. Typical teenagers. So you have to understand my horror, my total disbelief, and shock when not even just a year after school had finished that he committed suicide. I couldn't understand it, how could he do that? He had everything going for him, from my point of view, and yet here he had killed himself. What hope did I have, if he who had everything could end his life?

That's just it. Just because someone looks good, looks like a leader, looks like a manager, doesn't mean they should be, could be, or ought to be. Subsequently, I found out that behind the mask my friend held in front of him were massive family problems that impacted on his life. This is what really led to his demise.

Look, everyone of us has problems. As I mentioned before, there is no such thing as a perfect leader. We all have problems, whether they be personal or work related. And probably none of us looks like what we imagine a leader should look like, and maybe we don't even sound like what we think a leader should sound like. The first time I heard my voice I was horrified, and thought "That is horrible! Why would anyone want to listen to that voice?" Reality is that people are used to my voice because that's all they hear. They've never heard me speak differently. They don't hear the voice I hear in my head.

Look at yourself in the mirror. Go do it right now. What do you see? If you are a typical or average person, you will look in the mirror and you will begin to note the things you think are wrong about yourself - the hair (or lack of it), the height, the posture, the build, the clothes, the eyes....all sorts of things that you would notice - but did you notice the things that were good about you? And if you were to write them down, would the bad things make a longer list than the good things?

Now do something else. Go back over your list of bad things, and identify which ones are there because *you* see them, compared to the ones that others have told you about yourself. What do you see? For most of us, the 'bad' list is one we have made up ourselves. "My eyes are too close together" or "I should be taller" and so on. We even do this with how we speak, such thoughts as "I need to be more interesting" or even as I said "Why would people want to listen to this voice?"

You cannot judge who will be a leader by what they look like. Don't write yourself off just because you don't like what you see in the mirror. And don't compare yourself to what other leaders look like, because that's just not an effective measurement. To be a good leader, you need to be you. This doesn't mean that you shouldn't change anything about yourself - this is often where a good coach comes in handy. But it does mean that it's not about how you think you should be, it's about what you are now and where you want to be.

Look back in history. Napoleon was small of stature and apparently had a squint. Churchill was round and fat and balding. Golda Meir was anything but beautiful. John Howard doesn't look all that fantastic either, except for his famous eyebrows, nor does Julia Guillard look or sound good. Tony Abbot should never wear Speedos again. Yet they have all been or are or may in the future be leaders.

How you see yourself is important, because it has the power to stop you from becoming what you truly could be - or, it has the power to make you what you should and could be. Change your perspective. Change your attitude. Change your thinking. Don't assume you can't be a leader because you don't look or sound like one. It's just not true.

And one last piece of advice on this: don't compare yourself to other leaders. You aren't those other leaders, you are you, a unique individual who, whilst you might have some similarities to other leaders, or do things the same way someone else does, you are not a clone, you are uniquely you. Yes, learn from other leaders; yes, copy their process if it fits your style; yes, ask the questions of them and get as much learning as you can – but don't try and be someone you aren't, because firstly, it won't work because you aren't that other person, and secondly, people will instinctively know that you aren't being 'real' or 'true' to yourself. They will pick up that something is wrong, even if they can't put their finger on it, and that then strikes at your integrity.

CHAPTER 2
So start with commitment

We tend to only notice people once they have risen to the top of their profession. The big name speakers, the top athletes, the well-known leaders of countries, the bands and lead singers, we see them once they have arrived. But how did *they* get there? That's what I'm interested in. Because if I can see how they got there, I might be able to see how *I* can get there too. The problem is, once they have 'arrived', someone writes their biography, and usually what happened along the way either is embellished or lessons along the way get forgotten, or the accuracy of the memory becomes clouded. Listen to people talk about the past in a family get-together and you will see what I mean. Someone shares a story, another member says "That's not what happened" and now the fun begins. As they tell what happened, someone else chips in with a "I think you're forgetting..." and on it goes. That's to do with perception as well, but also what we sometimes call 'selective memory'. I choose to remember only the good parts, or the parts that affect me, or the things I want to hang on to.

So as I said, I want to know how they got there, because maybe I can get there too.

SO START WITH COMMITMENT

I have been working with various sports personalities over the past three years behind the scenes to help them achieve in certain areas in their lives, and it has given me an insight into one aspect of leadership from a different vantage point. Most of the athletes I have worked with are at the top of their field; they are alert, athletic, determined, and realistic (in the main). Realistic, because they know the toll their sport has taken and is continuing to take on their bodies. Having interviewed multiple numbers of our top athletes, the one question I have consistently asked is this one: "How come you made it? How come you made it, yet others around you, friends you had who must also have wanted to be the sort of athlete you are - they didn't make it? How come *you* made it?"

Without a doubt, the overwhelming response has been "commitment and determination". What do they mean by that?

Let's look at commitment first.

Their commitment was so real that when their friends went out partying, they went to training. Sometimes their friends would say "come on and join us, you've been working hard for the past few months, you need a break" they said "you go ahead, I'm going to training". Come Friday night and it would be "Let's go out for drinks" - except for these people, they would say "I've got training tomorrow and coach told us not to drink before practice" and the guys would say "Hey, it's just one night" but these athletes said they were determined to get into the squad, and the next day you could usually tell who had been 'out on the town'. They were committed to making this happen, and if that meant sacrificing having a good time or being out late with the mates, they chose to be committed to the task at hand.

My next question was to ask whether they still kept in contact with their old friends who never made it, and the sad reply was that, in most cases, they did not, because they now represented the one who had made it - and were a reminder to their friends that they hadn't.

The lessons learned here from these sports people could well be applied for us all. It is about commitment, even when you don't know the end result. Think of the player who sits on the bench week after week, not knowing if this is their week when they will be chosen. Yet they train the same as their teammates, they attend the same sessions, they are there every week, they do the same weights, run the same distance...it's about commitment. Commitment is not about waiting until you have been chosen and then being committed, it's about being committed before you get chosen and then showing that you shine once you have been chosen! Being chosen is usually a recognition of the commitment put into the training before it all comes together, and the only reason it comes together is because you were committed!

In all the interviewing I have done, it has never been about the school the person went to, the education they received, the wealth of the family, the position in the community or where they were born. People from the 'wrong side of the tracks' have often been at the top as well as those from rich heritages. The difference is not necessarily in the background; it's in the person and their level of commitment.

Think of the 2002 Winter Olympics and there's one Australian who comes to mind - Steven Bradbury, short track speed skater, representing Australia. He got into the finals due to the failure of several other skaters. He knew he would not do well, and his strategy (and his coach's) was to simply 'hang in there' and hope someone falls. Well, that's what happened in the semi-finals and Bradbury ended up in the finals. He was the slowest skater, and he knew it. Comes the final race, and he knows the rest of the bunch are far better than he is. In fact, it was always tipped that Apolo Anton Ohno, the American speed skater, was favoured to win. So much so that apparently Steven had said to Ohno (who he knew): "When you win, make sure you mention my skates" - Steven has a company that makes skates and he supplied them free to Ohno -

that's how sure people were that Ohno would win. Even Steven was sure of that. His strategy again was to hang out at the back of the pack in case someone fell, but reality was it was unlikely to happen at this high level.

So what happens? The unthinkable, really. The race begins and as expected, Steven is coming last - until the final lap, the winning lap, where one skater well in front of him clips the skates of another, both fall, taking out the others tightly bunched around them - except for Bradbury, who is well behind them. The only person left standing - is Steven. He slowly glides through the mass of bodies and crosses the finish line to win gold whilst behind him, bodies are scrambling, literally clawing and scrabbling their way across the ice to get to the finish line and at least get a placing. It is one of the most confusing moments of Winter Olympic history, even Steven himself not being sure what's going on. He looks totally bemused, almost as if he isn't quite aware of what's happened. Yes, other skaters put in a protest, but in the end, Steven won out.

What made it possible for Steven to win? Can we put this down simply to the fact that he was 'in the right place at the right time' as some people would say? Or is it something more? I'm going to suggest it is something more. Yes, in some ways he was in the right place at the right time - but we have to ask *why* he was in the right place at the right time. And I am going to suggest to you that it was because of all he had done up until that moment.

It was *commitment* that won Steven Bradbury the Gold Medal.

At any stage of his journey as a skater, he could have given up. The "I'm not going to make it so why should I keep on trying?" attitude, maybe not even making the effort to do the training. But he had done the training, he had qualified to be on the team, he wasn't seen as a serious contender for the race he was in, but he was committed. Committed to his team, committed to his cause, committed to do what he knew he could do and to do it as well as he could.

Steven actually had good reasons to give up. He had been in a serious accident on the ice in 1995 in Montreal where his thigh was slashed open by another skater's blade, losing massive amounts of blood and requiring a hundred stitches and redevelopment of his quadriceps muscles. In 2000, he broke two vertebrae in his neck whilst training and had to miss the 2000-1 season. Some people thought he would never skate again on a competitive level. When he returned the next season it was with the idea of competing in one last Winter Olympics in 2002.

At any time on this journey, he could have given up. He could have given up after his thigh and muscle were slashed. He could have given up when he broke his neck. He could have given up with all the hard training he was ordinarily doing, plus the additional work he had to put in after serious injury. All along the way, the thoughts must have come to him: it's too hard, it's too tiring, it's too dangerous, it's too demanding.....many excuses he could have come up with, but he was committed. I wonder how many people, whilst on the outside encouraging him, on the inside said "He'll never make it". Maybe Bradbury knew this, maybe he didn't, and maybe there were times when he felt like listening to the people who openly said this. But one thing is certain - he didn't give up, and history was made. He was at that time the only Australian - in fact, the only competitor from the Southern Hemisphere - to win a gold medal in such an event in the Winter Olympics ever!

In an interview afterwards, Bradbury made this comment: "Obviously I wasn't the fastest skater. I don't think I'll take the medal as the minute and a half of the race I actually won. *I'll take it as the last 12 years of hard slog I put in.*" That's commitment speaking.

Commitment. A really important basis for any good leader.

SO START WITH COMMITMENT

Determination comes hand in hand with commitment.

A good leader remains committed to the cause even though others may have given up on that cause. Commitment is different to determination, even though they go along together in the best leaders.

Together they make for a strong leader who gets things done. Together they make things happen. Although there are some similarities with both words, they are different enough to look at separately.

Commitment is about keeping to a decision made, pursuing the goal you had in mind. Determination is the strength to keep on going when all else fails. Commitment will carry you so far, determination takes you past the 'so far' to the outcome you want to achieve. Commitment gets you started, but determination helps you finish. Commitment is about cause; determination is about strength and continuance. That's what Steven Bradbury showed in his life to win that Olympic Gold.

Another example of this combination of commitment and determination is seen in one of the most controversial brain surgeons in Australia, Dr Charlie Teo. Dr Teo operates on people who have brain tumours when others refuse to do so. Many of the surgeons will say "this is inoperable" but Teo says there is no such thing as inoperable. He says that anything is operable, it's just the results that might be a concern. The fact that many surgeons even set a deadline - this person has only three months, that person six months, this one a year to live - this becomes an issue for Teo. His feeling is that we cannot and do not have the right to determine how long a person might or might not live. He believes that people often resign themselves to this prognosis and that belief becomes reality. Somehow the time limit given comes true. Although this verges on the whole area of positive thinking, there is enough evidence (of a kind, maybe not as scientific as some might want) to prove this a reality.

Teo's 'trade' was learned overseas, as he felt that the type of surgery - almost a surgery of hope - was being completely disregarded here in Australia. He learned new techniques overseas, and apparently pioneered neuroendoscopy for brain cancers and tumours. He then returned to Australia and attempted to implement it here. The problem for him was that he was - and still is - outspoken, and openly disagreed with his fellow surgeons. He was abrasive in manner, and had no problems in challenging the status quo. He was soon not welcome in many hospitals and operating theatres. He continued to go against the traditional approaches, and would operate when others wouldn't.

People began seeking him out as they heard about this miraculous surgeon. People who had been given a death sentence by other doctors, or their children had been given a death sentence, began to see Teo as their last hope. Because of all of this, many doctors refused to refer patients to him. In fact, some doctors actively dissuaded people from seeing him, some going as far as removing them from their books if they went ahead to see Teo.

There have been neurosurgeons who have criticised Teo as being radical and giving out a false hope of a cure to patients who they 'know' are going to die. Teo's continues to operate and care for the seemingly incurable because, as he says, he can. He is a much sought after speaker and surgeon overseas.

One mother here in Perth was happy to discuss with me her son's condition, a life-threatening brain tumour. The doctors had given up on him, said that all they could do was the chemotherapy without any guarantees of success but said they could expect him to die. So she turned to Dr Teo. She and her son flew over to the East Coast to talk with him, and to see if he could help and remove the tumour.

And here's an interesting thing. Dr Teo examined the young boy, and determined that it would not be right to operate, as the tumour was too close to vital structures, and he could not operate without causing severe and possibly fatal damage. His advice? Go home and continue doing what you are doing.

In another instance, Teo agreed to operate on a another young boy who had been given up on by the other specialists around him. This boy had been given six months to live (check out "Matthew's Fight for Life" on YouTube). Now, five years later, he is still going strong. Is he out of the woods? Not necessarily, but at the time of those clips he was still alive and enjoying a great life with only minor problems. Will the cancer come back? Possibly, and even probably, but he is still alive. Five years is certainly better than six months, wouldn't you say?

What's the lesson here, aside from commitment and determination?

The lesson here is to learn when to say yes - and when to say no, to not be so swallowed up by arrogance or 'blind faith' that you keep on going down the path you have chosen, even though it will end in disaster. The good leader knows when to keep persisting, but they also know when to stop 'flogging a dead horse'.

This is the other side of commitment and determination. You have to be really careful not to replace determination and commitment with arrogance and stubbornness. This is really hard, as people will assume that they are being determined when they are really being stubborn. Or they think they are being committed when in fact they are being arrogant. Sometimes we have to listen to other people and get their evaluation, because it is about perspective, being able to see from outside the situation. When you are in the middle of it, it's hard to see or be objective.

Some people never learn that. They are natural disasters, looking for somewhere to happen. They've done it before, they are committed and they are determined, and they just keep on going, even though all the pointers around them are saying "stop"!

Good leadership is not stupid leadership. It is not about proving yourself right in every circumstance. It is about knowing when to stop and let go because even you know, if you are honest, that it just isn't going to work out.

CHAPTER 3
Offering hope in the midst of hell

What Teo is also offering is hope. Hope is not certainty. Hope is about the *possibility* of something, that maybe this will work out and I am trusting that it will.

There are, if you like, two types of hope. There's the "I hope it's going to work out, have no idea as I am going in blind here, and you know, anything could happen - but let's hope it happens". That's one. The other is "I've followed the process, done what it says to do, followed the rules, and now let's hope it works out - all we can do is wait and see".

When we talk about hope in connection with leadership, we're talking about the second type of hope - done what we can, followed the process, and now we have to wait and see. We're not talking about blind hope that forges ahead with no direction, people following "...because I'm the leader!" and then crashing and burning. That is not acceptable leadership.

Teo offers hope. His comment is that we should never take hope away from people, that no one has the right to do that. I believe he is right. When hope goes, so does our future, our belief in anything and everything and everyone. When hope dies, we die. Teo's feeling is that even if the operation only gives another month, or six, or a year, that's one more month or six months or twelve months than they had before to be with the people they love and who love them. But to his credit, Teo also knows when to say no, as in the case of the young boy from Perth. Teo is recognised for his brilliance throughout the world in the medical profession - except in much of Australia.

Again, there is a lesson here for leaders as well. Although this may not be true for most of us (as it tends only to be with those who are publicly lauded), it comes under the 'tall poppy syndrome' that seems to be prevalent in much of Australia. It does happen in a smaller way in organisations. The lesson? Be prepared for people to oppose you once you start to become known as a leader. They won't point out the good things you do, but will surely talk up the seeming mistakes you make.

Why does this happen? It's about jealousy. If someone else gets the attention, people around feel slighted and react. They would say they were being protective, or were simply challenging what they know is not right - they may come up with a hundred other excuses, but when all is done and said, it is jealousy. People do not like to see others succeeding where they themselves have either failed, or missed seeing what they could have done or been themselves. Or maybe where they are no longer the centre of attention.

I have been told that seagulls hate difference. So it is said, if you tie a red ribbon around a seagull's leg and then let it loose, the others will attack it and eventually kill it, simply because it is different. One of the famous books of the 60's was a book called "Jonathon Livingstone Seagull". It's about a seagull who discovers that he can be different to the rest, discovers a different dimension he can live in. He begins to teach this to others, but is soon ostracised by the rest of the group because of this. They can't accept that he has discovered something they don't know about, refuse to believe in, and isn't part of their tradition. It's an interesting book, and yes, it engages in spiritual theory, but it gets the point across - don't be different because in the end, 'they' will get you.

That is unfortunately the same reaction that can exist in organisations today. Don't be different, do it our way, don't buck tradition.
Now here's the crunch. Sometimes that advice is accurate. The task of any leader is to determine whether the basis for the advice is based in ignorance, refusal to change, disregard of the problems at hand, blind arrogance, or maybe truth.

Fortunately, this usually only occurs with public leaders. Those of us who live within the confines of office space and work-related walls usually avoid this particular inspection and attack. However, having said this, unfortunately people in the workplace can often face this in smaller doses once office politics come into play.

In training, we often talk about 'UGRs' - unwritten ground rules. Every workplace has them, and any leader worth their salt will seek to know what they are before attempting to become a leader of change. The reason for this is that if you do not take them into account, it doesn't not matter how much commitment or determination you have, you will always be battling uphill against what will feel like 'unseen forces' over which you just can't get control. No matter what you try, it will seem an impossible task, and if you aren't aware of these UGRs, you will go crazy trying to work out what on earth is going on! No matter what you do, it will seem as if you are expending huge amounts of energy that should bring success, yet you won't achieve the goals you set out to, nor will you achieve long-lasting results.

In many ways, this is what Teo has been up against in his battle to achieve results in Australia. This doesn't mean he hasn't achieved, but he may not have achieved as much as he could have if he had taken the time to understand and maybe address the UGRs. However, we will never really know the truth of that, and because of Teo's character, he may well have identified them and ignored them and continued down the same path he has anyway.

The other question we have to ask at this point is whether once you have identified the UGRs, it will make any difference anyway. Maybe Teo has identified those. Maybe he has tried to address them. The problem comes when you have identified the UGRs and tried to address them and they won't change or accommodate you into them. You have to ask the question: do I still consider what I need or want to do important enough to stand against the UGRs? Teo has obviously made that decision and has to wear the outcomes of that decision. The other issue for Teo also is that it took him time to recognise those UGRs, so over time they became major issues, but also he looked at them and decided to either fight them or ignore them, both areas which came back to bite him. Now, he finds it difficult if not impossible to repair the damage that he caused by not identifying them in the first place. That's my read, by the way, based on his interviews and other people's comments.

So what can you do about the UGRs? Should you do anything about them once you have identified them, or are you doomed to live with them?

CHAPTER 4
Working with UGRs

How do I identify what the UGRs are? This is not an easy question; they aren't called 'unwritten ground rules' for no reason! This is the 'stuff' that seems to ebb and flow through an organisation, it's like seeing something out of the corner of your eye, yet when you look straight at it, it disappears. That is really frustrating, because you can't seem to grab hold of it, it melts before you get a good look at it!

UGRs are often only discovered when you cross them. They're a bit like the boundaries of your property - you sort of know where the edges of the property are, but usually the only indication of this is the four pegs that reside at the corner of the land. Sometimes people have discovered years later that the fence they thought marked the edges of their property were out; sometimes that has resulted in major or long-running court battles. UGRs are a bit like that - you can't see the actual lines, but crossing them can result in long term pain!

So how do we find them? Like the property, you may have to look for the 'corner pegs'. The corner pegs are the markers, the constants of the property. In any organisation, there will always be the people who 'know' what is really going on. Sometimes (but not always) they are those who have been there the longest. Not always, because sometimes the people who have been there a long time may have become the most cynical and even bitter, and if you dig deep enough, you will often find that they once had big dreams, visions of the future, of what could be, and tried to create change and it bit them.

So ask these questions: who has been there the longest? Who seem to be considered the 'go to' people - you know, when a question comes up, people say "Go talk to so-and-so, they'll be able to tell you".

A colleague of mine shared his personal experience. In one place of employment, he made the mistake of not checking the UGRs. He suggested to the Senior Manager who was instrumental in hiring him that he would need to feel his way in rather than jumping in feet first, but the manager said he wanted my friend to jump in and create change. But what about the other people around him, he asked, won't they be upset by this? To which the manager replied no, as they knew this was what my friend was employed for. They were expecting him to jump in feet first, he told my friend, so there won't be any surprises there. My friend listened to him. For once, he ignored the things he had learned about UGRs. After all, if anyone should know the ethos of the organisation, shouldn't this Senior Manager?

My friend said: "I don't think I have ever upset so many people at the one time in the one place in my life! Within about four weeks, I had alienated two of the major players who were instrumental in my being able to achieve what I had been employed to do, and because they were in the Senior Manager's ear each time I 'did something wrong', my relationship with that Senior Manager also took a beating. It took me all of twelve months to win back the support and confidence of the two major players - twelve hard months that could have been more productive in achieving the outcomes I had been hired to achieve, if only I had listened to that inner voice in the first place, telling me to check the UGRs. In fact, those two major players were two of the 'corner pegs' I should have been checking things out with. I didn't do my groundwork, I paid the price".

A hard lesson to learn. But, once you have learned it, it's not one you like to make again!

The question is, who are the major players, the 'key pegs' in your organisation, with whom you should be checking and creating working relationships? Do you know who they are? If you listen hard enough you will be able to determine who they are. They will be the ones to whom the CEO listens, or who influence the discussion, or at the end of the day seem to get what they want even though others don't.

Another organisation in which a different friend of mine worked many years ago had very devastating UGRs - a new person in the organisation very quickly formed a personal relationship with the Managing Director. Every person had a problem with the way the relationship played out to influence the UGRs. It was as if the whole dynamics of the organisation totally changed - and in one sense they did. Even to the point where someone didn't say good morning properly to this lady, and she was in the MDs office complaining. The next minute, the person who supposedly had not greeted the lady in the way she thought was appropriate (and her complaint was about the tone of voice in which the other person greeted her) was called into the MD's office and told to apologise! Many good and productive people left that organisation because the UGRs had changed and they didn't know it, and when they found out what they now were, they wouldn't stand for it. Certainly there was a moral issue here as well, but that wasn't the main reason why people left. It was the changing UGRs that undid them in the end.

From a leadership point of view, you do have to find out what the UGRs are, and then decide if you can work within them. You have the choice to work within the parameters of the UGRs, to ignore the UGRs, to try and change the UGRs, to try and influence those who set the UGRs, or bash your head against the

UGRs in continual conflict! Whichever choice you make, you have to be prepared to live with that choice and ensure it doesn't conflict with your basic values.

In the end, in the example I gave above with the CEO, the new person and their personal liaison, my friend was one of the many departed ones who left the organisation because the UGRs were totally unacceptable to them. Their values disallowed their continuance in that organisation.

Let's look at the different choices we listed.

Firstly, working within the parameters of the UGRs. Let's suppose you have found out the UGRs and they are very clear to you (usually you never discover them all, by the way, certainly not straight away), and you have identified the 'influencers' (people) who control them. The question you have to ask here is this: do your personal values allow you to accept and work within those parameters? Remember, not all UGRs are bad or immoral or impossible to work within. This is not a question of 'good and evil' here, rather it is one of whether you feel to work within them will cause you a conflict of values. No conflict, then you are on a safe journey, and you'll make it! It won't be easy, but you will survive.

The second choice is to ignore the UGRs. Many people believe that if they ignore them then they will go away, or they won't affect them, or maybe they can plot their own course and create their own UGRs. This is what we call 'pipe dreaming'. This phrase, by the way, has been suggested as coming from the opium dens in China in the 1800's, where the people who smoked the opium went into a dream-like trance, and believed incredible things, saw amazing things in their minds. They really had no possibility of ever coming true, but it seemed real and possible at the time. Whoever ignores the UGRs or attempts to just ride roughshod over them will reap the rewards of such a brave stand - and possibly one of the rewards will either be an unsuccessful work life, or the possibility of a new job somewhere else!

You can't ignore the UGRs. They are the basic fabric of what makes that workplace work. Ignoring the UGRs opens up the possibility that you will constantly be crashing against the UGRs and the undercurrent will possibly destroy you and your success. If you ignore them, you are more likely to constantly walk into them or trip over them.

The third idea was to change the UGRs. This is not as silly as it might sound, because at least it is recognising that the UGRs do indeed exist. The big question is: can you change the UGRs?

The answer to this is: yes you can. It also depends on several other things as well - what is your power base, whether the influencers of the UGRs are happy to allow you to change them, whether you can become one of the influencers, and time. Time is the killer, though. How long are you prepared to wait for that change to happen, because it could take years! Most people aren't prepared to wait that long.

You may be able to change the UGRs or at least affect them while you are the 'new kid on the block', but remember, you might have a 'honeymoon period' where it seems you can't do anything wrong. Take advantage of the honeymoon, it will soon wear off. The problem is, you might be able to affect some changes during this time, but you may find the influencers are prepared to wait until you make a mistake - and they will be the first to point out how you have messed up.

Next is to try and influence those who set the UGRs. This may be possible as long as those who set them are still there in the workplace. Some UGRs remain long after the influencers set them in place. The reason why this might happen is because the UGRs may give some advantages to certain positions or roles. Why would anyone want to give that up?

You can try and influence those who now control the UGRs, but this is not an easy one. It can be done. It means creating relationships with them, one-on-one time, but be aware of this: building the relationship has to be genuine otherwise they will know it, and you will be inviting big trouble on your head! Trust me, been there, done that...

Note that at first they may not believe you as you try to create that relationship, and that's why it will take time. Most influencers are very suspicious when people try to get alongside them. If you are in a hurry, don't do it. Be prepared to take the time, even years, before you can change the UGRs or influence those who set them.

The last one is often the norm - banging your head against the UGRs in continual conflict. Reality is, this one's not really an option at all that you should even consider, because it is a dead end choice. It will leave you frustrated and alone, and your work will become hell for you.

One Consultant on UGRs in Queensland (www.ugrs.net) specialises in addressing UGRs in companies. He says that to identify the UGRs, get people to ask "around here..." and you fill in the rest. For example, "around here, customers are..." or "around here, decisions are...". His comment is that if you ask this question of the staff, you will discover the UGRs.

UGRs are often what causes a feeling of disconnect in organisations. The values of the organisation may be written on the wall or distributed throughout the organisation or even spoken loudly by the management team, but if the UGRs are not aligned to the values, there will always be a feeling of disconnect, something will seem to be there that you just can't put your finger on. But you will 'feel' that there is indeed something there.

UGRs can also be positive, by the way. They aren't always negative in application. For example, the start time of an organisation might be 9.00am, but in this organisation people get there at 8.40am and prepare for work to officially start at 9.00am. Maybe the pre-9.00am arrival gives people the chance to grab their first coffee and chat around the coffee machine, maybe it simply allows people to clear their minds and get ready to go, but whatever it is, that's a UGR - people arrive early in this organisation, so it affects others and they too arrive early. That's a positive UGR.

Don't underestimate the power of UGRs. Discover them where you can, and work with them where you can. Whichever way, you will either have to try and influence them, or at the very least, be aware of them and work with or around them and the people who are the influencers of them.

CHAPTER 5
Good to great leaders

An article in 2011 June's BRW Magazine commented that in 2000, Jack Welch (GE CEO) was named the manager of the century by Fortune Magazine. He was often referred to as 'the CEO's CEO'. Now 10 years later, although he still travels and speaks and commands a huge fee, he's maybe out of date!

Welch was known for his tough stance, for removing waste and error at GE, as well as firing the bottom 10% of performers in GE. He believed that by getting rid of the bottom 10% of performers in the company, people would scramble over each other to ensure they weren't in that bottom section! One Management consultant and academic commented that Welch was obviously an exceptional leader, but times have changed and he is not seen as a leader for today by many people.

This consultant went on to say that employee engagement is a key motivator and is really the main job for any good manager. In fact, they contend that how employees and managers interact has radically changed from Welch's time, and recognition of what a person is and does is paramount for a good manager today. It means managers have to communicate a lot more and with higher clarity than ever before.

Communication - or the lack of it - is one of the biggest reasons why staff leave companies in Australia today. Many people assume it is about pay or not being a good place to work, but they're not the main reasons. Those reasons might come into play at some stage, but by far the largest turnover of staff is created by poor communication.

Research by the Gallup Group shows that the reason people leave their jobs is not so much about the organisation as it is about the manager they work for. In fact, a 2007 survey showed that 24% of employees would fire their boss if they had the chance!

So now we have two areas of concern to look at: communication and engagement. The research tells us that they both go hand in hand – that the lack of communication from manager to employee is what eventually causes disengagement. Again, this management consultant goes on to say that disengaged employees often feel that they are not valued or understood, they don't feel part of the decision making process, and they resent not receiving regular feedback from their immediate manager. Disengagement by employees can lead to non-completion of tasks, harassment, bullying, and low quality work, which costs the company.

One of the problems identified is the lack of what are called the 'soft skills' of managers. Most managers have been promoted because they have the technical skills and knowledge, but when it comes to the people skills, they have been found to be sadly lacking.

It's like the old story of the sergeant major who was told to ease up on his men, and had to tell one of them, Private Jones, that his father had died and do it gently, so he goes on the parade ground and says: "All those with fathers take one pace forward - not you Jones!"

Australians aren't good at giving feedback, or praise or recognition, whatever we want to call it. We are all aware of what has been called the 'tall poppy syndrome' which we have already mentioned, and something in our makeup gets us to lop the tops off people before they even get to be tall poppies anyway. Consider the 2011 winner, Jack Vidgen, of "Australia's Got Talent" fame - even before he got to the very finals and looked like he would be the winner, he was already receiving death threats! Hello! The kid's fifteen, for goodness sake! Well, we don't receive death threats in the workplace, but we do create death in people by how we don't give recognition. So we give praise, but then we take it away - here's a praise moment: "Well done, John, thanks for your help on the XYZ project, really appreciated - mind you, a blind man and his dog could have done it just as well". We give praise, and then we take it away.

It's not so much the *what* that is communicated as it is the *how*. How managers communicate to their employees is crucial. It's *how* we put the words together that counts.

Malcolm Gladwell is an author who has written several books (such as "Blink" and "The Tipping Point"). In one of his books, he points out the research done as to which doctors got sued and which didn't. He came up with some interesting facts. One such story he tells is about a lady who had breast cancer and it wasn't picked up until it had grown quite large. She wanted to sue the specialist who she was sent to see and who would operate on her. It was pointed out to her that he wasn't at fault, it was her local doctor who should have picked it up much earlier. She was the one who should be sued, she was told. "I'm not suing her," the woman replied. "I like her".

And that's the point: the discovery was that people sued dependent on their relationship with the person! The better the relationship, the less chance of a law suit. Maybe as leaders we need to learn from this, because the research shows us that the manager can be nearly incompetent and a bumbling idiot, but if they have a really good relationship with their employees, people will not only forgive them, they will support them and even hide their inability as a manager - simply because they like them! I have to admit, I take *great* comfort in that!

The Melbourne based company, Kronborg Leadership Advisors, says that employee engagement is no longer the sole responsibility of the HR department like it used to be. In 'the good old days', HR worked on this, and management and boards concentrated on the bottom line, the outcomes of the sales, and so on. Nowadays, KLA says, all managers need to realise that engagement and clear, good, positive communication is the responsibility of the good manager, and probably makes up the main focus of their role.

As KLA says, meaning and purpose have become the new currency in staff retention - in management training, we have always called this the WIIFM factor - the "what's in it for me?" question. Managers need to be able to help employees discover meaning in what they do, rather than people just turning up for work, putting in the hours, and then "re-engaging their brains" once they step out the front doors of the workplace.

Whilst this might all sound somewhat negative, let's look at the positives. Let's look at what managers need to do to captivate their employees and have an engaged workforce.

Firstly, it is about positive communication. At one stage, we used to teach people to use what we called 'the praise sandwich' - that's where you talk to an employee and tell them something good they are doing, then tell them what they are doing wrong, and then finish with another good thing. However, research tells us that when we have these conversations, and managers talk to staff and tell them something good, the staff are waiting for one word - anyone guess what the word is? "…but". You are correct. So now they are saying, split the two. Give good feedback when it is due, and give corrective feedback when it is due, and don't mix them.

Part of the reason for this as well is that Gen Y and the upcoming Generations are into coaching. Not sure if you realise it, but Gen Y is the biggest users of personal coaching ever. And you want to know the second biggest users? Baby Boomers.

So this is the next solution to keeping good staff - providing them coaching, not just placebo coaching, but where managers spend time helping Gen Y improve what they are doing and learning. Part of this makes sense when you look at it - Gen Y knows that their employability depends on their being able to do the best job, and they can only do that if they can be trained.

That's the next step - providing training for employees. Not just sending people on training for training's sake, but meaningful training. Planned and *meaningful* training tells a person they are worth something to the company. But beware, there is a sting in the tail on this one. It's not good enough to send people on training programs, *managers have to also support participants when they return to the workplace* to enable them to put into practice what they have learned.

In his book "Good to Great", Jim Collins poses what he calls 'Level 5 Leadership' which, he says, is not easily attainable for all. When asked in interviews whether people can learn Level 5 (L5) leadership, Collins is a little bit vague. He does, however, link this L5 leadership for the success of many top companies he and his team examined in great detail. This type of leader is about 'the team' rather than the CEO standing out as the saviour of the organisation. In the past, people such as Jack Welch (former CEO of General Electrics), or Lee Iacocca (former CEO of both Ford and Chrysler) or Kenneth Lay (former CEO of Enron) were held up as exceptional leaders who made their companies sing. Whenever they were reported in Time Magazine, or other financial papers, they were hailed as the answer to many problems. Even books written about (or by) them always had their photo on the front, because the company revolved around them, and 'how they did it'.

Now, we are a lot wiser. We have seen the shallowness of their style of leadership, whether or not they helped secure their respective companies financially - at first.

Now we know the financial problems they caused, the way they treated people (Welch's byline: "my way or the highway"), and that in some instances, they left the company in a worse financial state then when they started as CEO. The big question I ask people now when using these people as examples in the leadership area is to name who are the CEO's now for those companies - and you know what? Most times, people can't do it.

Collins would call this L5 leadership, where the CEO is not necessarily in the foreground as once was the case, but the team takes the credit. When the CEO is interviewed, it is about the collective 'we' rather than 'I'. This is not because the CEO is wearing a false cloak of humility, it is because he actually does recognise that he didn't do it alone.

There are two things here to take note of. Firstly, this type of leader ensures others get the recognition for the work. Secondly, it doesn't mean that the leader is being shy. This type of leader is not shy, nor are they humble as we think of that word. In fact, they do have an ego, and that ego is actually important for them to achieve what they do.

This is one of the problems I see with Level 5 leadership that Collins doesn't mention. People tend to think that leaders shouldn't have egos, that they should be kind, tender, loving, always smiling, giving, not ruthless, and humble. In reality, what we have described in that last sentence is probably a good description of a psychopath! That's how they come across.

Listen! True leadership is rough and hard. Yes, it does mean that a truly great leader considers others and compliments them, recognising their achievements to others rather than taking the credit to themselves. However, they can also have large egos, can be tough, ruthless, and yet caring at the same time. There seems to be an inconsistency in who they are and how they live that grates the average person. And they are not perfect.

Sometimes when teaching leadership, it is so easy to paint the picture of a good - or even great - leader as someone perfect, always making the right moves, constantly smiling, never firing people (or if they do, it's with great torment of the soul), but that is the incorrect picture. They still have to answer to a Board or Executive or even Shareholders at the end of the day, so the decisions they make have to take those to whom they answer into consideration.

Great day-to-day leaders are susceptible to the same peculiarities we all are. They feel pain, they get angry, they make mistakes, they make bad judgement calls - all the same things you and I do. So what makes them good or great leaders?

They are great leaders because they are prepared to take the risk. They also instil trust in and from people. They have worked their way to the top (I'm talking about the CEO's here) and so have a proven track record. They usually have integrity and work to strong principles.

Now what we have to realise here is that we may not always agree with the principles by which they live and breathe and work. That's why I think we have problems in trying to identify who is a Level 5 leader. We have this preconceived idea, and if someone doesn't meet that idea, we wipe them off as an L5 leader and relegate them to a 3 or 4. Every leader has their peculiarities, and we need to ensure that we don't fantasise about what this leader should look like. I have never met the perfect leader yet – and by perfect, I mean someone who doesn't make mistakes or has some idea stuck in their head that you just don't agree with as a follower of that leader.

But having said that, most of us are never going to be this type of leader. By this I mean the L5 CEO type leader. I have looked at what my CEO does, and I don't want that, thanks very much! I wouldn't survive. So where does that leave me? And where does it leave you?

This is where we have to identify some important issues about leadership.

CHAPTER 6
Is everyone a leader?

The current theory is that everyone can be a leader. That is both true and false.

Some years back, Prince Charles was visiting a school and listening to their essays about what they wanted to be when they grew up, he made headlines and got into a lot of trouble when he said that it was wrong to encourage every young person to dream of being Prime Minister of England (some three or four students had written that). He said it wasn't true, and that to say so was absolutely absurd.

People all over the UK and beyond absolutely crucified him and demanded a public apology. Why take away hope from young people, they cried. Let people aim at the highest office. Prince Charles, however, was right. He went on to explain his comments by saying that whilst it was a great ideal, realistically it was totally impossible because at any one time only one person could be Prime Minister! Therefore it might be that whilst we encourage everyone to aim high, we also have to be realistic - not everyone can be Prime Minister.

So too with us. Whilst we can aim at the highest position, we won't always get it. Not all of us can be CEO's of our company, because at any one time, only one person can be in that position. If it's me, it won't be you. If it's you, it won't be me. And if it's someone else, it won't be either of us.

But on the other hand, we can become leaders of something. Leaders in the area in which we work. If a leader is about aiming high, being the best I can be, living in integrity, creating a place of trust for people around me, giving my time to ensure what I do is of the highest standard - then I can do that. By attaining to the same standards we set our top leadership, we can be leaders.

But not necessarily leaders of the company...

That's what this is all about. It's not about how to become the top leader of the bunch. You need another book for that. This is about being the best you can be wherever you are. This is about real leadership. Because you CAN be the leader you should be. Not just a *good* leader, although your journey may start there, but a *great* leader. This is about being aware of the areas that don't get discussed in most leadership books.

So let's realise that we need to aim for the highest level of leadership we can, whilst also realising that we may not always get there. Let's also realise that whilst we strive for the highest, we may have to settle for a Level 3 or 4 in Collin's strata. Our problem could be that we see this as a 'lesser' role and become dissatisfied with what we achieve, rather than recognising that we are exactly where we should be. This doesn't mean that we shouldn't strive to do better; the key is recognising if we are where we should be.

These days, we have fantastic resources to help us in that identification. Kouzes and Posner, in their book "The Leadership Challenge", have a 360 degree questionnaire which helps people identify their leadership style is one example; Myers-Briggs is another resource, as is the Hermann Brain styles of thinking. Collins we have already mentioned, and Marcus Buckingham is another writer whose books are well worthwhile considering in the leadership arena.

Buckingham, in fact, proposes an interesting thesis - that we should not be concentrating so much on our *weaknesses* as much as we should on our *strengths*.

This becomes a fascinating discussion for all managers, because you have to admit, he has a good point. In his book "Go Put Your Strengths to Work", Buckingham challenges the 'everyone can be a leader' concept. He also challenges the idea that we should identify our weaknesses and work on them. His thought is that we were never hired because of our weaknesses, rather we were hired because of our strengths. Someone looked at us and said: "We like what this person has to offer" and therefore we got hired. So, reasons Buckingham, why do we then, once we have been hired, start to work on our weaknesses and ignore our strengths - the very thing for which we were hired? Why would we not work on our strengths, to make them better?

Buckingham has a fantastic point here that we ignore at our peril. I don't think he is saying that we should totally ignore our weaknesses, but he is certainly saying that we shouldn't ignore our strengths. While we concentrate on our weaknesses and spend time improving them, our strengths may well suffer, and in the end we appear as if we have lost our original passion and attraction that once drew management to hire us.

This is why it is so important that we know who we are meant to be as a leader. And what makes us one. If we don't, we will forever be trying to live up to an image that isn't real, and forever frustrated.

This is why it is also important that you recognise who you *are* and who you are *meant to be*, so that you don't try to become what you are *not!*

This can often be the trouble with performance reviews, in that they are spent telling us what we a re not good at, rather than helping us focus on what we need to become. In fact, performance reviews should focus more on our strengths and how the organisation we work for can help us to enlarge those strengths, rather than telling us what we aren't doing well.

Performance reviews should only highlight the areas of weakness that are preventing our strengths from being utilised properly. The idea should be that we are helping a person develop their strengths more, and we are identifying for and with them the very things that stop their strengths from being at their peak. If we could focus on this, performance reviews would become viewed by people as a very positive experience, rather than the annual "this is what the company thinks of you" usual approach, which tends to devastate everyone around them including the person running the review.

Again, some fantastic books have been written about this, so I am not going to repeat what can easily be read elsewhere – this is to get you thinking about the value of what you do when you review someone's role in your area or department. After all, this may well be something that you do have control over and are able to affect by your example.

IS EVERYONE A LEADER?

I know for myself, my 'annual review' is anything but something to be feared. My immediate manager takes me out to lunch and we have a very informal discussion about what I feel I have achieved in the past year, anything that I would like to see myself doing in the next year, what personal development I would like to engage in, and then I am introduced to anything that the Institute would like me to do in the next year as well. This last one isn't presented as something I have to do and their decision is already made – it might be, for all I know – but the manager talks it through with me and asks how I feel about it – I have input into this. Because I trust this person, I am prepared to listen, give input, and then take on the task. If the task seems daunting, I say so, and we talk it through before I am committed to it.

Performance reviews need to be what they were originally designed for – to enable a person to become the leader they ought to be. How you handle a performance review will tell everyone what kind of a leader you really are. Good leaders find this annual review to be a fantastic opportunity to lead their team members into the future.

Fortunately for us, it is becoming more popular to have several reviews throughout the year, rather than waiting for one time in the yearly calendar to check performance. Again, good leaders hold many individual meetings as well as team meetings to determine where people are at, and to redirect if necessary. By doing this, we can help each person on our team to 'strengthen their strengths' so-to speak, and be more effective in their role - and ultimately, in what they are producing for the company in which they work – and for you as their leader.

CHAPTER 7

Where does a leader get their power from?

I want to address the issue of power. Whenever we talk about leaders, people always think of position and power. So let's talk about some of the issues here.

Firstly position. Look, there are different considerations here. Although some people think immediately of 'front of the pack' when you say 'leader', this is not always so. A leader can lead from many different positions that yes, does include leading from the front. But a leader can also lead from within the pack. What we are talking about is where the person is and what power they have. Any good manager knows that somewhere in their staff on the floor is someone who has what we call 'influence'. People listen to them. When there is an issue, people naturally turn to that person to ask them what they think. In that sense, that person is a leader. They may not have been elected by the hierarchy, they may not even be the Team Leader in an official sense, but they are the leader. A good manager will realise this and work with them to achieve. Simply saying that they won't use this person because they don't hold any position isn't going to cut the cake. If you recognise that this person is essential for your smooth flow of the work, you can get the positive support you need; on the other hand, ignore them because you didn't choose them, and they will lead anyway, but now it might be from a very negative perspective.

Position can be an influence. But it could be limited influence. For example, a politician has influence, and the more important the position they have the more influence they have and the more people want to be around them. The problem obviously arises when the politician loses their next election or retires or ends up as the Opposition. Then people will desert them in droves. Whilst the politician holds that position, however, they have power and influence. But keep in mind that it's not a power that lasts.

I like the identification of power that the conductor of the Boston Philharmonic Orchestra, Ben Zander, gives to leadership. Ben and his wife have written a fantastic book called "The Art of Possibility" in which Ben talks about the leader and power. He talks about his discovery he made when he was in his 40's that the conductor is the only person in the whole orchestra who doesn't make a sound. The conductor, Ben maintains, uses his ability to make other people powerful. That's where he gets his power from. He says that he looks for what he calls 'shining eyes', and if he doesn't see them, he asks himself what he is not doing that their eyes are not shining.

I love his description of leadership. It really sums up a great philosophy that is partly captured by Collins and Buckingham in their respective books. Empowering others really is the role of the great leader, and empowering others is what gives the leader their own power.

Power is not something that can be grabbed. Some people think that they have to force themselves into a position of power, but that is far from the truth. Force works both ways, and there is always someone stronger who can come along and force you out of the position into which you had just forced yourself! Colonel Gaddafi has found that out, as are many other Eastern country leaders of recent internal upheavals.

So if I read Ben Zander correctly, he is saying that the leader's role is to make other people powerful. Another way of saying this is that the great leader empowers the other person, they work on helping that person to become what they could and should become. They see the potential in a person and want to develop that potential, whether or not the other person sees it as well. It's about helping people to become.

This is so much more powerful than force. Do you know why? It's because force works only for as long you have that powerful position. Once that position changes, disappears, or you are removed from it, that's when you can tell if the person was a true leader. If they are not a true leader, people will desert them, because they were only following either because of what that leader could do for them, or because of fear, fear of what that leader could do if they weren't following them. The problem with forceful leadership is that you can't control what the follower thinks or does when you are not there to watch them.

A leader gains their power when they serve others. That's what it really comes down to in the end. Some leaders lead by force, but that is not lasting unless you are a dictator of a country in some isolated area - but these days, even that is becoming more precarious! When you serve others, you make them shine, and as they shine, they grow and take on true responsibility. As *they* do so and achieve, *you* achieve. It's not about racing ahead of the mob and waiting for them to catch up, it's about being with them, growing them, encouraging them, and empowering them. As someone once said, if you want to know if you are a leader, look behind and see if anyone is following you. If they are, you're probably a leader. If there isn't anyone following you, then you're simply going for a walk.

So we have the potential for two areas of positioning – the position of power, and the position of influence.

WHERE DOES A LEADER GET THEIR POWER FROM?

Dictators use power as the means to move people. They are definitely not serving people. This means that in the background there is always the possibility of revolution. What starts a revolution? In most cases, it is about the misuse of power. Look at the many Eastern countries today that are having problems with their rulers trying to maintain power by crushing the opposition with force. Depending on the courage of people in those countries, there is always the possibility of uprising as people begin to feel that they have had enough of being downtrodden or ignored.

Zander maintains that power is OK if it is used to make the others around you powerful. In this way, he encourages people to develop what some in the past have called 'servant leadership'. This approach encourages the leader to look for ways to help people develop and display their strengths for the greater good of not just the individual, but also for the group as a whole. I think that part of Zander's ability to do this is because he is working with a group of musicians. It can be easier to see if a group of musicians are in harmony, working together to produce music, than a group of people who are producing goods on a production line.

It's about getting the orchestra to work together and using each individual strength to produce music whereby no other instrument outshines or overpowers the other – they play to their required strengths and produce beautiful music. You can 'hear' the beauty in the combined strengths on display – but you can also hear the discord if someone is too heavy in their playing, or is behind or ahead of the others.

Zander is the conductor. He has discovered that his position of power comes from making the other players in the orchestra powerful individually and collectively.

A position of influence can be as above, or it can be from within the group. A conductor stands out the front and waves their arms about. You see the power in their strong sweep of arms and baton to increase the volume, or the smaller, condensed movements closer to the body as they subdue the orchestra to reduce the volume. In a position of influence, you might see the above, but often it comes from within the group.

Sometimes we see that within a group or department there is a manager, but that manager doesn't always 'call the shots'. Somehow, there is another shady figure that we just can't put our finger on who really dictates what is going on. This is often aligned with the person who has set the UGR's – they're there, and we know they're there, and they are the people that others look to and who really set the agenda. We talk about 'hidden agendas' – this is where that really comes into play.

People may have that position of influence because they have been there a long time and people listen to them because of their wisdom. Or they may have that position because they listen and get things done. As with power, this can be misused and become destructive in any organisation. If you have people like this in your group or team, get alongside them, turn them to your way of thinking so that they begin to work with you rather than against you. It can be done.

As leaders, I believe that we need both of the above – the position of power, and the position of influence.

So where do we start? If you are a 'newbie' in the organisation, it can be hard to start to create change. You need both attributes to succeed, and you need people who have the above to help you make the success happen.

When I first created a totally different program to what the Institute was used to presenting, I received a lot of negative comments as to whether it would work or not. One thing I have learned is to not take those comments personally. Why?

"People hate change around here" is something you may hear from time to time, to excuse why everything remains the same.

Let me let you into a secret. Whilst this might be true, it is more true to recognise that it is the fear of the unknown in change that affects people most. It's not the change that people usually react to (some do because they're comfortable, but most don't), it's the fear of the unknown associated with that change that affects people most. It's not knowing how that change is going to affect me personally, that's the big worry most of us have when change is announced. Will it affect my role? Will it change my responsibilities? Will it affect my wage? Will it impact on my time? Do I have to move? These are just some of the questions that people will have in their minds and usually not ask – they don't want to be seen as against change, especially if it comes from higher up, but they are questions that we need to address, just the same. Often when people react, they are not reacting to you, they are reacting to the possibility of how it affects them, whatever 'it' might be.

So when I created a new style of delivery for one particular program, it did get the negative comments to start with, and I wasn't prepared for them – I hadn't written this book yet! But fortunately, my manager had a lot more wisdom than I did, and his advice to me was to find a consultant who would be interested in running the program as I wanted it run, as I had envisioned it to be, and then get them on board. I think this is what Collins is also referring to when he says that we need to 'get the right people on the bus'. One consultant came to me and asked if he could run the program using the materials I had developed. I said yes. This consultant was someone who had influence, and once they took it on board, ran it, discovered that it worked and worked well, they became a very willing and loud advocate of this new program – and it began to take off. I credit its eventual success to this consultant's ability to see the good in the change, not be afraid of it, and to take it and run with it and then on-sell it to others by virtue of his very verbal support and encouragement to others to become involved, which they did.

So good leadership, great leadership, is about recognising your position of power and influence, but also recognising those around you who also have one or other or both of the above, and utilising their support, energy and enthusiasm to get other people involved and on board as well. However, it must start with one person – you. And this is what Zander is talking about when he says that the leader's role is to empower others.

CHAPTER 8

Where have I come from, where am I going?

This is one chapter you might want to miss. This chapter has some very spiritual overtones to it and most Australians are not very comfortable discussing this area of their lives. We have reacted to the over-emphasis that Americans give it, and the stiff upper lip not discussed (it's your private affair) British style of handling things, and come out on the side of the cynical and sarcastic self-effacing approach that typifies us as a country. Sport has become our god, and our sports people are amongst the highest paid in our country (depending on which sport, of course).

I was talking to one of the sports officers attached to a well-known Sports Club, and he commented that in his opinion, sports people should be role models, and instead they have become (not all, but in larger numbers than people want to admit) selfish, obnoxious, self-opinionated, over-paid demi-gods, allowed to get away with almost everything because they are sportspeople. He was hoping that somehow, sports people today could change this image and create something good. Let's hope he's right, but only the future will tell. Because it's sure not happening at the moment.

So this leaves us with the terrible question: why do we have so much issue with a spiritual belief system as being important or part of our lives? Some of our problem goes back to the founding of Australia, which was deliberately set up as an opposite to both the British and American society of the time. The idea was to set up a society where Government and the Church were not bound together as they are in both the US and UK. Overall, they succeeded.

We have also based our Western society on the teachings of some of the early Greek philosophers thoughts and ideals. One of them promoted very much the five senses - hearing, touching, feeling, tasting, and smelling. Another, on the other hand, had the five senses but added a sixth sense, the spiritual dimension. One famous film, "The Sixth Sense" was based on this premise, that there is another dimension. More and more films have surfaced that deal with this hidden area, because it intrigues people on the one hand, even though on the other hand they ignore it in their own lives. Some philosophers taught that there was 'another world' that lived alongside our world, which encompassed this sixth sense. Some, however, asserted that this world was all we had. Both took their concepts further than this, but this is enough to give you the basic idea of their teaching. Interestingly enough, the East has followed the six sense thoughts whereas the Western world has followed the five sense thoughts. So in the Eastern world, no one blinks an eye to see religion as part of our day to day living, whereas in the West we tend to shy away from public displays of either religion or emotion.

The reason this area is so important is that it can determine our direction, our end goals, our ethics, our determination to achieve. It can also affect how we see other people, how we see our job, and how we relate to others around us. If you believe in this other dimension, this spiritual side of mankind, then it has a tremendous impact on how we live. It also impacts how we don't live.

From a leadership point of view it is important because it should determine how we lead people, how we consider them - are they simply pawns on the giant chessboard of life, or does each person have meaning? If they are pawns, who cares? Tread on them as much as you like. If there is meaning for each person, their job needs to take that into account, otherwise you won't get the best out of them, and then you as a leader or manager can't achieve required outcomes and outputs.

We also have to face reality here in that religious beliefs, ethics and ideals don't necessarily mean people treat other people better. It should, but it doesn't. That's why we have had so-called religious wars where the very worst has come out of people in what they have done to others in the name of religion. Or people who have a huge belief in conservation, may err on the side of the trees rather than a man's livelihood, or an animal liberationist might march for the animal yet condemn the person mistreating the animal without the realisation as to why that might be occurring, because it's the only way he can make his meagre living to support his family.

This in no way is written to say either side is right or wrong, but rather to make us genuinely look beneath the surface and see the truth and deal with it, even if we have to put off what our intention was when we first started the crusade.

So our understanding of this spiritual side of man is important if we desire to lead them to an end goal. One major reason is that the spiritual intensity, which I happen to believe is inbuilt into all of us although possibly expressed differently, has to be satisfied for us to feel we have succeeded. The journey might be hard, and the emotional toll might be exhaustive, but if we feel satisfied spiritually, then we will be more accepting of the situation and we will hang in there longer rather than back out when things get hard.

In leadership, we call this 'achieving buy in'. Once someone has 'bought' into the concept we are trying to sell, they begin to own it. Once they own it and are convinced on the value of what we are trying to achieve, they will move heaven and earth to get there - not because you asked them to (although that might pull weight if your boss or CEO is behind the ask) but because they now own it, want it, desire it, are living and breathing it.

In one sense Australia is not a hugely spiritual country, not in the sense that permeates some other countries like India, Malaysia, Bhutan, Indonesia or Tibet - these countries are extremely spiritual in their approach to life. Our spirituality has become more internal on the whole, although there is a significant rise amongst the youth of our country in spiritual searching, which makes sense if you think that for the past years we have been desperately trying to eradicate anything spiritual. Having the major denominations constantly highlighted in the media because of child molestation has not helped, as it has made people feast on the dirty washing of religion, and wipe all spiritual ideals off rather than recognise that this is actually through every area of society, not just a religious issue.

Be that as it may, the fact is that to *not* recognise that there is a spiritual side of a person is to ignore a major part of a person's makeup. You can't lead them if you only recognise 2/3rds of a person.

I don't want to make a big issue of this here, but I do want to make the point that this spiritual side of a person may be part of their strengths and weaknesses and therefore has to be taken into account when we lead people.

George Bush Junior is probably one of the worst examples (in my opinion) of a leader with seemingly spiritual convictions. A famous story is told of when Bush's advisors were suggesting a path of action, and the then President Bush decided to ignore his advisors and put forward another plan of action because he had 'prayed about it and sought God's wisdom on it' and 'felt' this was the way to go. I am going to suggest that this is an example of spirituality gone wrong, and that instead of being spiritual, it was more arrogant than anything else.

Again, these are some of the problems people have with spirituality, because they look at the worst examples to prove their point.

In all seriousness, we will always find bad examples of both spiritual and non-spiritual people and decisions made by those leaders, and that's simply because at the end of the day, we are all human. We make mistakes. Some people overeat, but that doesn't stop the rest of us from eating. Some people over-spiritualise, but it shouldn't stop us from considering the spiritual aspect of man.

Maybe this could be a great time for you to have a spiritual check-up....

CHAPTER 9

Values, Ethics and Morality and the leader

Inevitably, if we are serious about leadership, we have to discuss ethics. Before we do this, let me give you two scenarios - both true situations - to think about.

On the 15th May, 2006, a British climber by the name of David Sharp died on the slopes of Mt Everest. When he was eventually brought down, and the tragedy examined, it was discovered that more than 40 other climbers had passed him by as they made their way to the top - and not one of them stopped to help him. It was observed by all who passed by that Sharp was unconscious but breathing.

What would you have done? Would you have helped him? I talked to someone who had been training over the past 2 years to climb Everest. His comment was that you only have a limited supply of oxygen, food, medical supplies and so on, worked out to the last detail because as you get higher it is harder to carry materials with you. Also, he added, there is only a small window of opportunity in which to climb Everest because of the weather, and you may not get to climb it again for years. His comment was: do you put aside all those plans and money and training to help someone who may not survive anyway?

Apparently there are some 170+ bodies scattered over the ascent to Everest, although recently there have been plans for a team to try and recover them. Again, many of these people died as other climbers passed them by. No one stopped to help.

Second scenario. In contrast, on the 26th May, 2006 (11 days later after Sharp's death), an Australian climber, Lincoln Hall, almost died on the same climb. Hall had made the climb to the top and was now on his descent. He was alive and lucid, but unable to move anymore. Lincoln suffered a form of altitude sickness, and the team with him had diminished oxygen supplies. They were ordered by their expedition leader at base camp to leave him and return to camp as it was becoming too dangerous with the closing weather conditions and they were putting their own lives in danger. 12 hours later, the next morning, another team on their way up discovered Hall and abandoned their attempt to climb Everest, saying that the mountain would still be there another time for them to climb, whereas Hall wouldn't be.

Now the team, Hall's team, had returned to base the day before (25th) and had already sent out a message to the media and his family that Hall had died on his way down the mountain. When they left him, they knew that he would not survive the night on the mountain without oxygen supplies and in the extreme cold, so to them he was already dead.

This is where ethics and morality come into play.

Ethics is usually considered to be the set of rules or principles that guide or determine the actions of a person or group of people.

Morality is about right or wrong conduct.

Ethics comes first, and then morality follows after - if you like, ethics gives principle, whereas morality gives action based on principle. Ethics is about the philosophy behind, whereas morality is the practice.

This has come to light over the past few years with the superb crash of companies in the US such as Lehman Brothers, or Enron, to name but two. What has been concerning for Universities and Business Schools such as Harvard, or Stanford, is that some of the top players in such companies were their graduates! So they have become more aware of the whole ethics situation, so much so that it has become a major and compulsory subject for all its students for the future. And the reality is that as you examine the reasons why these and other companies crashed and were shown to have no substance, you do have to ask what happened to ethics? It was all about making people wealthy, about ripping people off without remorse.

This whole issue is now beginning to affect the Australian business as well. As people start in employment, especially Generation Y, they become concerned as to the ethics of the companies for which they work. Are they sustainable companies? Do they support the whole green philosophy? Do they care for and support countries where famine is rife, education low, and child workers exploited?

So the wise leader has to question and check their ethical base in today's age. And therein lies the problem.

Not all problems have simple answers. You may be aware or not, that in risk management there are two matrices that people check when a problem arises. There is what we call the 'likelihood table' and the 'consequence' table.

Likelihood looks at how often something might happen. Consequence looks at the impact of what might happen. Likelihood says that something will happen regularly or seldom, whereas consequence asks what financial penalty might be levied against the company and what kind of news coverage it will get.

Organisations these days are very conscious of their identity and public image. With the rise of social media, any issues with a company very quickly become known by huge numbers of people, which is why it is sometimes said that something has 'gone viral'. So consequence is very real for organisations.

Coming back to the instance of Mt Everest, we have to ask what ethics and morality were involved here. The problem for us is this: most of us reading this will never have climbed Mt Everest. In that sense we can never truly appreciate the impact or decisions made in these circumstances. It is very easy for us to sit back and say what they should have done. That's because we aren't doing it, and we are making a decision from the comfort of our armchair. It's worthwhile going onto YouTube to check out Mt Everest and the deaths and risks. One clip mentions a disaster on the mountain and how another group had to deal with it, people being carried down or stumbling into the tents for help. One such person had another female climber on his back as he tried to make his way back. Part of the way along, she slipped off his back because she couldn't hold on anymore. And he didn't have the strength to be able to lift, carry or drag her along, so he had to leave her there whilst he made his way down to safety.

On the other hand, another climber from New Zealand stayed with his friend and fellow climber who was in severe trouble further up the climb, and refused to leave him, even though he knew the risk involved - and as it happened, they both died. They were all from the same group, and that day, 17 people died in the fierce storms.

So which one was right? The one who stayed with his friend and died, or the one who left the female climber and made his way to safety?

This is where people would question each individual's ethics. On what basis were the decisions made? Why did one stay with their fellow climber whilst the other left theirs? All were with the same team. All would have discussed these and other possible scenarios and identified what they would so in such and such a situation. Yet when the crunch came...

The Aspen Institute is an interesting organisation that researches in these and other areas. In a survey they conducted in 2001, 2002 amongst MBA students, they discovered that when it came to the ethical decisions students were encountering in the workplace, there could sometimes be a difference between what a student said they believed, and what their actual response was when they faced such decisions. In fact, some of them almost 'lay down and surrendered' as they accepted that it was impossible to stand against the demands of the organisation. They weren't happy with it, but they had an almost fatalistic acceptance. They felt they couldn't change it. Aspen concluded that the end result and success in this was about choosing to speak up, or not. The question they then asked, of course, was what helped people to make that choice to speak up? Or not speak up?

Some of what they discovered was interesting - well, all of it was, but we will only look at a couple of things. They discovered that past experience made a difference, for example. If someone spoke up in the past and was listened to, this influenced how they reacted in the future under similar situations. Well, not everyone has those past experiences, and this is where they discovered their next key - that when people practiced and discussed what they would, could or should do before it even happened, this helped when they faced a real situation similar to what they had talked or enacted through.

One of the key people presenting in this area at Aspen and in partnership with Yale is Mary Gentile. She has written an excellent book called "Giving Voice to Values", which is the term she uses. This has become a major and apparently mandatory course for all MBA students.

Gentile argues that values are different to ethics and morality. She contends that ethics are about rules and principles, whereas values are personally held beliefs. I think she is right. Values probably determine our ability to agree or not agree with ethics, which leads to morality. Gentile again argues that morality is different to values, because morality is about what's right or what's wrong, whereas values are more about belief held deep, and therefore affect our morality.

Two Princeton University psychologists, John Darley and Daniel Batson, ran an interesting study with theology students which was based on the Biblical story of the Good Samaritan. The Biblical story goes that a traveler was attacked by robbers and left for dead - he wasn't, but he was badly wounded. Along comes a priest, and this man goes quickly past. He doesn't want to risk the chance that the robbers might still be around. Another man comes past, a Levite this time. He too passes quickly past. Now this is interesting because a priest in the old Biblical times was supposed to stand between man and God, and to represent God's character and presence to His people. The Levite was also in the priestly group but was possibly a lower paid official in the church, also sometimes having a political role to play as well as a spiritual one. A Samaritan comes along and helps – and in those days, the Samaritans and Jews absolutely hated each other and would have nothing to do with each other.

So these two psychologists decided to try and replicate this story but in a modern day context. They asked a group of upcoming theologians to prepare a talk on a theme they gave them (they met individually) and go to another building to present that talk. On the way, they had prepared someone to be lying in an alley, groaning as if attacked. To some of the students, before they left to go to the other building, they said "Hey you better hurry, as I think you're going to be late!" and this had an immense effect on them. Of these 'late' students, only 10% stopped to help the poor guy lying in the alleyway. Of the other students who had a bit more time, 63% of them stopped to help.

When you think about this, it is really incredible. These were theological students, so you would think that the story of the Samaritan would be known to them. At the very least, the ideals of the Bible should have had some impact, one would think.

This tells us what happens when stress is applied in any form. What we think we believe may well go out the door, and what are our real values comes to the fore. Our values determine whether we can follow the ethical standards set out by an organisation, whether we will then apply moral standards as well.

As a leader, you need to make your values very clear. We cannot determine the values of the people on Mt

Everest that fateful day, because we weren't there. We do, however, need to be very clear as to our own personal values. At which point will we say no, or at which point will we turn our heads away and pretend we don't see? At what point will we speak up?

Our values must align with the values of the organisation where we work; otherwise we will be in internal conflict or even external and public conflict.

Leaders have to be very clear about what they value, and they have to 'sell' that to the people who follow them. It is our values that attract people. They align with them, they identify with them. They begin to espouse them. So check your values, because you will soon see people around you who begin to look very familiar - like you, in fact. That's because they will be, because they will have absorbed your values.

And check the values of the organisation for which you work. If their values don't align with your values, consider going somewhere else. Unless you have the power to change the values, find another company, because it will eventually destroy you if your values differ more and more from that company. Remember, the values of the company will determine the real ethics, and the ethics will eventually be displayed in the morality around you – the right and wrong.

At the end of the day, the mission statement can sound grand and fantastic, but it is the values that count for what's real in the organisation.

Values count more than mission statements.

CHAPTER 10
What can I really do?

One of the reasons why the spiritual side of a person is important is that I can use it to help me identify what someone can or can't really do. My spiritual side gives me direction in my life. By looking at the past, I can (to some extent) identify my future. What do I mean by that?

I have done many things in the past, I have learned different skills, increased my knowledge in areas I once knew nothing about. As I look back on the collective experiences and learnings, I find that each new journey I made in regards to jobs or roles I have held brings together the sum total of those parts and utilises the bits and pieces of skills and knowledge to create a new understanding of my future. Let me give you an example.

These are some of the 'bits and pieces' of learning, of various skills and knowledge from the past in my life. I have at various times done film editing, photography, drawing, helped write a program to run overseas, spoken at youth camps, given a devotion, had an interest in music, written a play in a moment of inspiration, taken on doing graphic art for concerts for a charity group, and worked in a homeless shelter.

I've also worked in the church, led worship, worked with problem students in schools, taught a series on communication at a local College, been a chaplain/counsellor to a Mining College, started a youth group, pastored several churches, spoken for a series of programs on several radio stations, and presented on television. I have also trained many people as an independent trainer and consultant, worked within the TAFE system, and written a novel. All of these are totally separate events, fully disparate in content and application, individual events that have nothing to do with each other - until I look at where I am now.

My present role commits me to training people who sometimes don't want to be there. So I have to ask the question: what is it that can do that would attract people to the training programs I run or develop? How do I ensure that learning actually happens? This is where my past comes into play to create my now.

Working with problem students made me look at alternate ways to get through to them. The normal school education system was useless in their life, and they were disruptive, to say the least. Coupled with this, one of the students I worked with had personal issues, especially with male teachers. Unbeknownst to these teachers, one particular male student was being regularly molested by his father, so any physical touch by a male teacher was regarded by this student as abuse, or possibly leading to abuse. So in the midst of confrontation, for a male teacher to put their hand on this young man's shoulder in an attempt to calm him down led to disaster. I was asked to work with him, as the school psychologist had too many students to work with, and needed support, and I was seen as the one to take this on. I decided to get him involved in two things: the first one was martial arts, a one-on-one session with a friend of mine who taught this. The second one which I knew I could work on was teaching him how to play squash. Both sports involve physical contact, but physical contact of a different nature - you have to touch and grab in martial arts, and even have close physical contact as you work on moves in slow motion. In squash, teaching someone how to serve, how to hold the racquet, again involves touch, but also playing on the court has the possibility of running into each other. That's part of the fun! I had to look at alternate ways such as these to get through to these students who would not accept ordinary or 'normal' approaches. It was highly successful, simply because I was using a different approach than the norm, which had failed every time.

So I think that it is a leader's responsibility to find alternate ways to get the job done. This means looking beyond the ordinary ways of doing, to the extraordinary ways instead. And this is what we need to do here. It is also why we must not ignore the spiritual aspect of a person or society.

I do believe in the spiritual side of mankind. I am myself a spiritual man, and believe very strongly in the hand of God in our lives. I also think we would be surprised at how many other people also feel the same way. They may not believe in the same God I do, they may call their god by another name, maybe they only believe in an "essence of being" or something like this, but this belief is definitely there for many if not most people. What might differ, however, is whether people believe in a *personal* god who works in their lives. I do believe in that, and therefore this influences how I see myself in leadership. I believe that God has a big part in what happens in my life and in the outcomes I achieve; also that many of the things I have done in my life come together to make me what I am today.

So let's have a look at this. Let me take the different things I mentioned earlier and bring them together.

My current role allows me - in fact, encourages me - to be creative. Fortunately, as I have previously mentioned, my CEO recognises this part of my makeup and has put me in several different situations to allow me to pursue this side of my talent. But the question remains: how did I get here?

Well, look back at the things I have done in my life - the things in the past that I mentioned. They all seem disconnected, and if you take them as individual events, they are disconnected. In fact, if each 'event' was a dot, they could be seen like a vast dot disconnect, with no meaning, no pattern, nothing but a series of meaningless and disconnected events. Like this:

.   .

.

.   .

.   .   .

.   .

.   .

If each of the above dots is an event, what do you see? You're right, a series of unconnected dots. Nothing connecting them, right? So hold the book up, tilt it away from you - keep your eyes on the dots - keep tilting, until the page becomes less of a page and more of a slim segment or oblong. What do you see? If you are tilting the page correctly, you will note that the dots seem to move closer together, and in fact start to form more of a line - the distance between the dots diminishes, and they all seem to now head in the same direction, all seem to be on the same axis. In fact, some will even seem to be on top of each other. Now you get this, something that looks like a nice logical progression:

• ••• • •   • • • • •• •   • •   •   ••• •

But tilt the page back to how we would normally view a page, and it becomes a random cluster of dots again, unconnected, uninspiring, no story to tell. Well, in reality, every dot is a story, every dot is connected even when we can't see it. It's all about perspective, the angle from which you observe or look.

So I piece together writing a story, add in having to work on how to communicate on radio to an unseen crowd and inspire them, add in working with difficult youth who need a different approach to learning, some graphic art, some photography, music and drawing, and you have an idea of what I am doing today. I design new programs, totally different to what the Institute has run with before. I design the way it looks, the way the content is presented, the posters that go on display, even creating games for the programs, and working out alternative ways to develop a learning that will inspire people who may not want to be there! In other words, all the bits and pieces of my past now come together to make me, and make me successful in what I am currently doing.

So what is it that you have been doing in your life, your past? Have you ever looked at it all, all those disparate dots, and recognised the pattern they create? Maybe you have to change perspective, tilt the book of life a bit, until you see the pattern that makes up your life. It's worthwhile doing, because you may begin to see direction, see the way your life is heading, and identify what you should do next.

Every one of use needs direction, whether we call it spiritual or not. As a leader, I need to identify and acknowledge this. In some of our training programs, we have had to set a room aside for prayers where we have had people from overseas of a particular faith that sets time aside each day for prayer. This may soon become a part of the workplace, too.

In his address to new students at Stanford in 2005, the late Steve Jobs said about all he had done in his life, all the different things, that "...*you can't connect the dots looking forward; you can only connect them looking backwards. So you have to trust that the dots will somehow connect in your future*".

Take time to connect the dots...

CHAPTER 11
Have lunch with your future

When I first joined the Institute, Patrick Cullen, the Executive Director (ED), said to me "When we get to the end of your first year, I'll take you out to lunch to see how you are finding things". The end of the first year came, I went to lunch first with the Deputy Director who had been responsible for my being hired, and he went through how I had been from the Institute's perspective (which wasn't at all positive). In fact, I knew it wasn't going to be all positive because of comments along the way, and I was actually sure I was going to hear that maybe I should look for another job elsewhere - so sure was I, that I decided I might as well enjoy 'my last meal' (like the condemned man before execution) and ordered a beautiful three course meal, including lobster and prawns on a succulent steak!

Then the ED took me out for lunch and talked to me about the mistakes I had made, how he had seen me overcome them (although he wasn't sure how I had won some of the people over), and where he saw my future in the Institute. This gave me an absolutely fantastic overview of the Institute from the most senior person's point-of-view, which proved to be invaluable as I set about my future. In fact, I made a decision there and then that this was something I needed to continue. Fortunately, the ED gave me the opportunity by a throw away comment of "We'll have to do this in a year's time and see if you still feel the same".

The next year, I had this in mind when I sent Patrick a lunch invitation that pretty well said: "Remember the comment you made about catching up in a years time? It's come, so can I invite you to take me out to lunch?" and he did. So far, we have done this each year I have been at the Institute, all of ten years. Think of that: that's ten individual meetings with my ED, no one else around, just the two of us, and the chance for me to ask those burning questions. These lunches have averaged about two hours each time. That's two hours times ten which adds up to 200 hours or 25 work days of time. Imagine the value of spending 25 days with your CEO/ED where you get to ask all the questions you have ever wanted to ask.

I also learned to send him two or three questions beforehand that I was going to ask him, so that he would have time to think about them and give me answers that had time put into them.

These times have proven to be some of the most valuable of my working life at the Institute. They have helped me determine what I should concentrate on over the coming year, and ensured that I can align myself with where the Institute is going. What could be more valuable than that? It's like being given the game plan before the game even starts.

So why don't more people do this? Why don't you? I can hear it now, comments such as "I don't think our CEO would do this" or "You have to be kidding! My CEO doesn't even know who I am!" Well, he will after you have lunch with him. What's the worst that could happen? They could say no. But what if they said yes? Would you not jump at the chance? Of course you would! So again I say, what have you got to lose? At least have a go at it, and if you don't want to start with your CEO, start with your immediate manager, or supervisor, or team leader, and work your way up. Maybe it won't be lunch, maybe it will be coffee or something, but it's worth the try.

That's how I got to know some really remarkable people in my life. One day I realised something: maybe everyone makes assumptions that the top people, the successful people, even the famous people, are too busy to meet individuals like myself, but maybe everyone thinks this, and because of it, these top people sometimes sit in their hotel rooms alone, wishing they could go out and be normal like anyone else. One day I decided to test this theory and see what happened. I reasoned that I had nothing to lose, especially if it was someone I didn't know, who wasn't likely to impact my life at work. I could afford to take that risk as I wasn't likely to see them again anyway.

I was living down the South West of WA at this stage, and a very big Conference was due to occur, one that I was going to attend. One of the main speakers was someone I respected (from a distance) and would very much appreciate learning from, but how to find out how to approach him? I found out where he was staying, and during the Conference I rang his hotel and asked to speak to him. Lo and behold, I was put through to his room! I said I was at the Conference, and that I would appreciate some time with him, and would he be available for lunch the next day? To my shock, he said yes, he would love to do this, as he had free time, and no, no one else had thought to ask him out for lunch. Not every minute of his day was as planned as I thought it would be for a major Conference speaker. We had lunch, I asked questions, and it was a talk that placed me on a pathway that was to change my life.

What if I hadn't made this approach? What if I did what everyone else does - determined in my mind that he would be too busy and have no time for someone of my insignificance? That he would already be so booked up that he would have no time for anything else?

This is how I came to meet such people as Cliff Richard, Noel Paul Stookey (of Peter, Paul and Mary fame), or Dr Paul Yonggi Cho, Pastor of the largest church in the world (over 1 million members), Dr Robert Schuller of positive thinking fame, a previous Governor General of Australia, Colin Urquhart, one of the foremost theologians of our time, the Lord Mayor of Coventry where my wife and I became honorary citizens, a Senior Superintendent of New Scotland Yard, and many, many others who have added greatly to my personal growth - simply by taking the opportunity to make the approach because no one else did. Don't listen to those who always say "It can't be done" because many times it can be done if you have the courage to attempt it.

We spend so much of our life talking ourselves out of things that could greatly influence and change our lives, simply because we don't think it could happen for us. Unfortunately, there are plenty of people around who will also join in to talk you out of things as well, so why would you join them in putting yourself down?

There is the age-old story of a man who decided to mow his lawn, but realised that his lawnmower wasn't working, so he decided to go to his neighbour and ask to borrow his. As he walked, he began to think to himself: "You know, I loaned Bob my hedge clippers last month so I hope he lets me borrow his lawnmower" and he walked a bit slower. Then he thought: "Bob doesn't usually like loaning out stuff, maybe he will be pretty grumpy about it and refuse to let me have his lawnmower". He slowed down a bit more, thinking "Knowing Bob, he's probably going to be mad at me if I ask him for is lawnmower, he'll probably yell at me and slam his door in my face" and as he kept on walking over to Bob's place, he started to get annoyed. After all, he reasoned, why should Bob be so upset? He'd borrowed things before and always returned them in good shape. And anyway, he'd loaned Bob plenty of stuff before now!

By the time he got to Bob's place, he was roaring mad! He pounded on Bob's door, and when Bob answered the door, he yelled at him "I wouldn't borrow your stinking lawnmower if you were the last person on earth to have one!" and slammed the door shut in Bob's startled face and stormed off.

Silly story, I know, but it makes the point - we often self-talk ourselves into a place of unbelief and failure, even though we haven't even given ourselves a chance to pursue the ideals we thought we once might have had.

So why not invite your future out to lunch today? You never know what might be ahead with the knowledge you gain from that lunch.

CHAPTER 12
Mixing generations

We have never lived in such a time as we do now. We now have four generations in the workplace, and some (very few) might even have five! That means that we now bring different values, understandings and approaches to the collective table of what we call the workplace, and it means that we even more have to really understand the people we are leading. Even as we speak (or read, in this instance!), we are watching the arrival of an even newer generation that may really stuff things up!

I spoke recently to a colleague of mine who said to me "I don't believe in all this generational stuff – I think it is just a bunch of fairy stories to excuse problem people" so I asked him the following questions: do you find some of your younger staff find it harder to fit in with the general ethos where you work? Do you find sometimes some younger staff never seem to finish their work, moving to another task before they complete the first one? Do you have staff who either leave earlier than others or exactly on time, who also come in bang on time or slightly late? He replied: "I sure do! It's a real problem. I just can't find committed staff like I used to". He's got a generational problem, whether he likes to admit it or not.

So. We have the demise from the workplace of the Traditional Generation, the over 70's; Baby Boomers (BB's) are beginning their homeward trek of retirement with some already pulling their caravans into the sunset around Australia; Gen X are taking on the leadership and management challenge at work when the BB's let them - many BB's are still hanging in there as the Government encourages them to stay in work longer; Gen Y are vying for the leadership roles now because they don't want to wait around until they're 'old enough', and the Alpha or Z Generation is poised ready to launch into a workplace setting or go to University, and we have yet to identify what the Feral Generation will do!

One thing is sure, the span between the Generations is lessening, mainly because of technology. Between the Traditional and the Baby Boomers there was a good 20 - 30 year span; now between Gen X and Gen Y lies about 10 -15 years and then maybe 8 - 10 years to Gen Z or Alpha and maybe even less to Feral (Feral being born about 2001 on).

If you are a traditional identifier of the Generations, you will probably disagree with me and would lump the last two Generations I mentioned into one group. Some even group the Gen Y into the same as well and call them all Millennials. However, there is good reason why I would see this differently, and that really is because of the technology. Although a generation used to be considered the time between a person's birth and when they have their first child (which used to be when they were about 20 to 25), now people are marrying later in life and may not have their first child until they are in their 30's or even into their 40's! This then changes the way that we look at how we measure the Generation span, and it is now considered more accurate (or easier) to look at the technology.

Technology is on a speed rush at the moment. Believe it or not, this actually started with the space race back when Kennedy was President of the United States. Although this was about beating the Russians, the growth of technology stems back to that time. Considered a waste of money by many at the time, the amount of medical developments, increase in technology (because it was needed for the space program), and other benefits which have actually benefited mankind around the globe can be traced directly back to that venture.

When President Kennedy announced the race to the moon (actually pushed by Vice President Johnson and started in Eisenhower's time), there was no idea of the cost. Kennedy nearly had a fit when he was told it would be in the vicinity of US$20 billion! That was an enormous price back in the 60's, and hard to justify. However, at that time, the Americans thought they had no choice, as the Russians had already launched their famous Sputnik satellite which had beamed back noises to them - this meant the possibility of the Russians being able to work on this and send back meaningful information as their satellites spied on America and the rest of the world from outer space.

What that space race has returned to us in measurable benefits is the question we must ask. In fact, the return has been hugely immeasurable for mankind.

It created the start of the communications improvement revolution - satellite technology had to be created, which then meant the development of the computer on a smaller size, and from this the integrated circuit was born which would revolutionise computer technology; GPS and LandSat came out of this race, as has the condensed dry space food, which became important when used in impoverished countries or where famine struck as far as transport of food was required. It also increased medical technology that in turn revolutionised medical advances and experiments that would later improve how medicine advanced in the world.

That US$20 billion has since been trebled, quadrupled, even multiplied tenfold or thirtyfold and more as far as benefits to the world go, although not foreseen at that time.

Now we live in a world that is accelerating in what it develops. No sooner does a new product come out, when plans are leaked that a newer and better and more advanced version is already on its way. At the writing of this, we are already looking to the iPhone 5, iPad 3, and just recently announced, light transfer technology to replace wireless, which is anticipated to speed up the communication transfer process to more that 5 times faster than wireless. Maybe by the time you read this, that technology will be discarded for something else.

That technology is set to invade your workplace. How will you handle it, adapt to it, utilise it so that it makes sense in your space? And more importantly, who will be in your office to understand and use the new technology? Generation Z and Feral, that's who! So it is important to ensure you make room for that generation now. If you wait until they are in your workplace, it will be too late, because you then have to get the technology in that they have grown up with and is a natural part of their environment - until they come to your workplace and find it isn't there.

At a recent business technology expo in Sydney, Optus Chief Executive Paul O'Sullivan commented on a report commissioned by the Telco into the changing face of technology in the workplace, and confirmed that trends such as tele-working, the use of social media at work, integrating personal gadgets like iPad or Blackberry tablets into office networks was a major issue they were working on. He mentioned that their surveys showed that over the next three years, the workplace would see the number of personal tablets people bring in and expect to work with their work servers going from 25% to 55%. Not only that, but O'Sullivan also commented that some companies were planning to provide Twitter access or other social medium for staff, and that they estimated this would grow from the current 4% to 23% in the next three years.

That's when they will leave. Not because they don't like you, or your workplace, but because their realisation is that they have to keep themselves current or they themselves will be out-of-date and therefore unemployable!

We are actually talking about different life experiences. For example, Baby Boomers on the whole were raised mainly in a traditional family setting - Dad the bread winner, Mum the house wife, several siblings, dinner at the table, and make sure you have a clean handkerchief in your pocket when you go out. Gen Y is often made up of single kids, dinner at different times and not in the dining room, raised by two working parents, sometimes of the same gender.

Just those factors alone give different life experiences, creating two different Generations – and that's what we mean by Generational differences – we're talking about the context of the lives we lead in the environment of the moment.

But we're also talking *values and ideals*. Values and ideals are often created through contact with several different influences in our lives. They are also created and/or influenced by the social events in the world today and tomorrow.

So as leaders, we need to consider the future and the new Generations coming through. And the technology.

We will need to train the new Generations in simple things such as etiquette, whether it be at the dinner table or with office environment. Let me give you two examples.

One new program AIM has begun is called Emerging Leaders. This is a 4-day residential program for upcoming leaders in their workplace, and they have to be nominated by their managers for them to attend. What's interesting is that one session occurs over a formal dinner. The session is about networking, but it is also about table etiquette - the 'how to' of dining, what cutlery to use, how to leave your serviette when you get up from the table, and so on. Do you know what the etiquette is of the simple bread roll? No? So how will you go in a formal business dinner, especially if entertaining clients who do know the etiquette? In fact, at our last program, one of the participants shared how their CEO takes out his senior upcoming leaders to a restaurant and teaches them these very things because, as he said, one day they will be representing his company with some very senior clients, and he wants them to represent the company well.

Why would we bother? Surely that's the domain of the parents bringing up their children to teach them such things? Actually no. It's your job as the leader. Think on this: many of the younger generation have grown up with not sitting at the table for dinner. They may sit in front of the TV, or more realistically, take their food to their room and eat whilst they either study or watch TV. They shouldn't do that? What example do we set them in the workplace when we take lunch at our desks rather than taking a break? For the new Generation, that's the comparison they make.

Another example. We will need to teach what's acceptable and what's not in manners in the workplace. Just recently, a Baby Boomer shared their experience from their workplace, where they was having a private (or so they thought) conversation with a friend, and when this worker hung up the phone another younger worker spoke up and suggested that they had a solution for the issue that had just been discussed on the phone!

This older person was incensed, firstly that this person had been listening in and immediately offered a solution without saying something like "I couldn't help overhearing..." or something similar, and secondly that this person who was almost a third of his age would suggest that they had the answer assuming that the older and more experienced person didn't. Now whether or not they did have the answer is immaterial. What is important is the ideal behind what happened.

Think of the social networking phenomenon that is most widely used by the younger generation - Facebook. On Facebook, every conversation is pretty well in the open unless you send a secret message to someone. Most comments are simply sprayed onto the page for all to see and comment upon. This younger person was simply following the Facebook protocol - when you 'hear' someone else's conversation and you want to comment on it - you do. They were taking Facebook from one dimension - the computer page - and applying it to another dimension - real time in the workplace, face-to-face.

The other part of the situation was the Generation of the younger person in this instance - what is one of the things that Gen Y is famous for? Research. They will search the Internet for all the information on a given subject, and come up with various ideas of what could be done. Why do they do this? Because for Gen Y, information is success, power, fulfilment, and the way forward. They recognise that their value is in what they know, or in how to find what they need to know. Their whole future, as far as they see it, is dependent on information. That's what makes them employable, so to them it's pretty important to show what they know, and to show it fast.

So in this instance, this Gen Y person's suggestions make sense. They weren't really being rude or suggesting that the older person didn't know anything, they were simply following through and doing what they knew best - interacting on a visual Facebook level and finding and giving information. That's what they do best. My question is: how will the older generation react to this approach, if they don't understand what's really going on?

There's a lot more on generations that we could look at, but there are really enough books written on this subject to last beyond your or my lifetime, so look for them and read them, they could be well worth the read. Or go online and research it - or find a Gen Y in your office and get them to research it - they'll probably do it a lot quicker!

CHAPTER 13
Keeping good people

The last issue to deal with is this whole issue of engagement in the workplace that we touched on earlier. Startling results of surveys show us that just because people come to work doesn't mean that they are engaged in what they are doing. Apparently Australia is being shown up in the area of satisfaction in the workplace. I know that our organisation conducts staff surveys annually to determine how staff see the Institute and managers, and a plan of action is then developed to change what can be changed. Not many organisations do this, or if they do, they only do part of it but develop no action plan.

Again, as mentioned earlier, some surveys have the non-engagement of employees as high as 38%, and that is a huge percentage of disengaged people. Of those disengaged people, approximately 18% were identified as being actively disengaged, which meant that they were actively seeking to influence others around them against the very company in which they work!

This compared with American statistics in a survey completed by Gallup in 2007, where the disengaged were higher (some 56%), but the actively disengaged was also 18%, the same as in Australia. Their other statistic was also enlightening, that some 24% of employees would sack their boss if given the chance!

Why is that? Why would people say such an awful thing? Remember, more than 1/3rd of our day is spent at work, so that's a real indictment on our workplaces - and our managers.

It's about recognition. It has been recognised that those in leadership do not give enough recognition to their people. Another word for recognition is praise. We tend not to use the word praise much as it seems to carry overtones of over-the-top, almost (and I hate to say it) an American style of empty recognition. We have to be careful, though, because this is a cultural thing as well. The American over-the-top praise is fine - in America. It's expected, it's appropriate - it's cultural. We, on the other hand, are a halfway mix between the American and the English approach. Because of the English heritage, recognition or praise comes hard to us, and because of that, many employees suffer.

The question any leader should ask is this: what does it cost to praise someone?

It costs nothing. If a leader says it costs pride, or that people around them know they do a good job and don't need to be told, that person really needs to question their leadership. They might be a leader, but definitely they are not a good leader, and absolutely nowhere near being a great leader under Collins' definition! Great leaders, Level 5 leaders, are people who totally recognise the people they lead, giving credit where due. Not in a soppy or demeaning way, but in a genuine and enthusiastic way which tells people they are really meaning it.

In fact, the question a leader should really be asking at this point is: what does it cost to not praise someone? That is more to the point.

The cost is immeasurable. People will stay longer and do additional work for a manager or leader they know appreciates their work. Whether it is a "Thanks for helping out" or a simple handshake, it is very much appreciated. It's not all about being paid more money, although sometimes that might be required. It is about recognising a person's worth because of what they contribute to the organisation. It is also about not taking people for granted. Good leaders don't take people for granted.

A Swedish study found that the best leaders or managers who were considerate and who recognised their employees had a health impact on them. It indicated that people working for such leaders had at least a 20% lower risk of having a heart attack.

Collins mentions in his book "Good to Great" that it is important to, as he says, get the right people on the bus. What he means by this is that once you have the right people in your organisation, you can go anywhere you want to.

Well, it is your responsibility to not just get the right people, but to also keep the right people by treating them the right way. That is the way of the great leader. And once we begin to treat people the right way, we may be surprised to find that they are the right people we need anyway.

So it's your turn now, your turn to decide where you go from here. You can take the ideas we have talked about here and run with them, or ignore it all and continue the same you have before.

Run with them. Change the world. Change yourself. You'll never regret it. It's time. Now. Run.

About the author

Gene's parents and family were born in India, but immigrated to Australia in 1948 before he was born. Gene grew up in a family where stories were constantly told and relived of the family upbringing and adventures in India. This led to Gene writing stories and articles and eventually this book on leadership.

Gene has worked at the Australian Institute of Management Western Australia for more than 10 years, but his overall work life experience covers more than 42 years. During his time at AIM, he has specialised in creating unique programs based on a different style of learning. These programs often receive rave reviews and continue to be some of the premium programs the Institute offers.

Gene is a sought after speaker at Conferences and seminars on leadership, management, and working with different generations in the workplace. He is especially aware of the need to train young people and develop them as leaders of the future and commits his spare time in developing educational programs to meet that need.

He writes in his other spare time and is the author of a recently released teen's novel "With the Fear, Goes the Night".